Mustering What's Left

Selected & New Poems

1976 – 2017

Roger Aplon

Published by Unsolicited Press

www.unsolicitedpress.com

Copyright © 2018 Roger Aplon

All Rights Reserved.

Unsolicited Press Books are distributed to the trade by Ingram.

ISBN: 978-1-947021-18-1

Front cover design: Kiersten Armstrong, KMW studio

Photograph: Raymond Forget

Font: Adobe Caslon Pro

To

The Editors & Publishers who thought enough of these poems

to place them between covers honoring them

with their imprint

For

Debra Kaye

who vigorously encouraged this compilation

&

In memory of my Father, Carl Aplon,

who never acknowledged the importance of poetry

but to whom I owe an unpaid debt of gratitude

Introduction

This collection (ranging over 40 years), should be visited as a 'history,' a partial investigation of one writer's evolution. Many of the early poems (especially – *The Monologues*) were cursed, celebrated, maligned &/but eventually acknowledged as 'in the spirit of their time'.

Which, it should be noted, is in keeping with my intent as a writer: to capture in image & tenor an impressionistic rendering of the color & character of the world as I've experienced it.

That said, never being at ease with a single, limited 'voice,' I found myself exploring a different tone of 'voice' with each subsequent volume.

From the *monological* explorations in *Stiletto* to the impressionistic responses to contemporary music in *Improvisations* the rhythms & images I've chosen were meant to encourage the curious reader to respond viscerally – maybe touching a nerve that might otherwise remain innocent.

R A

Poems

From The Man With His Back To The Room (2006)

From

Stiletto

1 9 7 6

1

If Your Skin

If your skin were fine sand
I'd burrow
to the bone
planting apples for the morning.

If your skin were slate
I'd chisel leaves
& branches
bowed with yellow blossoms.

If your skin were moss
I'd drift in the tendrils
sleep between your ribs
with the drowsy snails.

If your skin were oil of cobalt blue
I'd scribble fingers
with long strokes
up & down the breathing of your spine.

If your skin were field grass
I'd rake the cuttings gently
sucking down
the faint odor of rain.

If your skin were rivers
I'd bob for crayfish in the pools
rescue quail & white peacocks
from the flooded banks.

If your skin were air
I'd conjure bats to glide
mercilessly
through the waves of tiny flying eyes.

If your skin were ice
I'd wrap you in the womb of a wolf
stroking her belly
with oil of mulberry & eucalyptus.

If your skin
under my hands
almost iridescent
in this dark room
reached warming

your sealed, secret, supple
skin . . .

I Call Her Name

Her face is a razor
stropped keen in dark barley.

Her hands are combs
cleaning dust from quicksilver.
She's alone in her house of hair.

Her cunt's a wasp
she flutters her hips to call
small children from the dead lagoon.

She's a wolf whining.
Green quirts sing in the corral
where she prowls, her skin invisible.

She bursts on me like glass
blown in the oven of a mouth
sucking the cock of a goat.

She shits incognito.
Behind the barn of her fine breasts
retrievers masturbate in silk socks.

She's a boot
sipping mud at each stitch, luminous
as butter, fat as dandelions.
She seduces corn.
Her silent nails tattoo butterflies
in the nostrils of buffalo.

Her thighs are walls.

I call her name.
She hustles my groceries in moving vans.

I call her name.
I demand an answer in her meat.
She must fuck the monkeys of Toledo.
I call her name.
She's hidden in the glove of a dancer.
She's riding the roads with a light colonel.

She will not answer.
No grenade can tear her from her new supper.

Watch Out

Over my eyes

the fat spring

leaves spill and the street

tilts its mouth

so full of glass

& grins back

to me at the corner,

I wonder how long it will take

to walk this block with its 17 people that I know

    The sun peppers the cement with tiny dimes
    and the twelve yellow numbers, eyes begin
    to shinny up the windows

I have 344 more steps to the other corner and another 389 steps
to the next corner after that and another 401 steps in the next
block to the next corner after that and another 3 . . .

(an eye [blue] stops at my right shoulder
but if i turn my head . . .)

    the beggar stares down deep
    to the bottom of his cup

There's a cut on the back of my right index finger
1 watch it grow
2 holes, I watch

the diamondback curls over the ledge watching me watch my finger begin
to thinly slip open a little more and drip a little more blood and it watches
me watch it on the ledge begin to coil away to the grey grass between the
slabs of slate and there are 2 holes on the back of my index and there is and
now the silver oil begins to circle the 2 holes

only 6 left to pass, counting—
146 147 . . .

      there's 1 (brown) eye in the air to my left
      there're 2 (green) beside the rear wheel of a '63

they all look and they
(there are only 61 steps)

      see me count my way to the corner
      and i think how tight i am
      in my black galoshes.

All My Life . . .

. . . in a minute d'judge'll come an do me
m'I a fool
sittin here
all shut down . . .
why now
all my life
I fought
all my life
til now . . .
deese fuzz mine me a mass
an d'tag-along brothas
wouldn't tink twice den bout
splittin a bad scene . . .
maybe I figure somethin out
it's too big t'hustle usual
you gotta have a scam t'match da odds
dey heavy an dey know da score
. . . if I jus cool it an pretend . . .
d'las time I did dis way
I's in the back a d'man's car
he thought I's *the babe in the woods*
t'hear him talk
never miss'd his gun
talkin

all t'way t'hell

wonder if dey figger dat one

an me doin time for rippin off some ol' dude

I's a stron yun dude

an tha's a fa't

If I's t'cop a plea

dey's mos like t'pass

an if dey burn me

I got ways

all my life

I got ways . . .

One

I could always swim in the big winter waves
or slide through the shrubs
hiding my face in my hands.
I grew my own food
in the place my mother hid me.
On dark nights I'd wind down
following the dim light of the river
and crouch at the edge of the town.
I once came close to a house
and heard the song a small girl sang
as she rocked her brother in her arms.

.   .

They came to me one winter
holding hands in the snow.
They didn't seem to be afraid.
They only asked for a place to stay.
We shared berries and the bread they'd brought.
That was years ago.
I've taught them the secret of riding the waves
and how to speak with their eyes.
I especially love the sounds they make
When their bodies touch.

Five

We make a cradle of our bodies
lying in each other's lap
rocking. The small waves barely hum
against the struts of the old pier.
It's no accident
we've chosen this high place
where the sounds of the gulls ripen
and the wind rests easily at sunset.
At night we can be invisible
the only hint of our presence
your raised breast glowing
in my hand
your thighs hugging
my cock into you.
We hold our breath just
for a second
listen for the kiss
of the huge goldfish
who've begun to move toward us
over the moss-covered stones.

A Christmas Present

I'm on a high-backed sofa in the Al-La-Deen, got a scotch
n'water working an another on the table. There's this chick
doing the popcorn tryin t'get her tights straight an a off-duty
priest sluggin on a warm beer. The bartender's drying a glass
when the door opens an in walks this Amazon 6 feet if she's
an inch.She's got this long, shiny black hair that looks like
combed tar an when she takes the seat cross from me I bout
shit. The bartender comes round t'get her order for a gin
over while I light the cigarette she's squeezin an pushin with
lips that work like bellows. We got it together, I think, when
she leans down with this big grin an starts t'shimmy from the
seat reeel slow, til she's up all the wayan reachin for this
switch −The next thing I know, she's got her hair offan she's
hangin it over a chair, an then her lips, an nose, an . . . she
keeps takin it all apart an layin it down til there ain't nothin
left cept her eyes lookin up from the palm a one hand, an I
see the priest's asleep an the bartender's readin the scores
so I gulp my scotch t'make it when this mouth comes off the
table growlin "where in hell you goin with my new toy?"

From

By Dawn's Early Light At 120 Miles Per Hour

1 9 8 3

Radar

For Karin Epperlein

First
her suicide was first
something disallowed inside the heart.

She is young
has learned early
the art
of positioning her body
to manipulate her legs
walk on her hands
parade her naked hips
upside down
to make us partners.

**

My body wants to leap cartwheel flip
I decry pretense
will be irrevocably exposed
at one with the surf
only the moon to guide the tides.
I'll be drenched in sweat

14

and the sweet musk of the coconut
a juice as unique as my own.

**

Her sisters arrive
pass out knives
adjust their machines
connect the wires
load the guns
fill the rubber bags w/blood.

This is their solo
And I'm their witness
someone to hold the props.
When they plug in the wires
it's my signal to bleed.
I've learned to be brave
encourage them
it's been agreed.

**

I shower and rest.
Mother is upset.
She brings my robe.
I drink a cup of juice
joke with the horny stagehands.

I will die two more times tonight.
I do this willingly
watch the audience
flick my small wet tongue
entice
the real killers.

The last will be in water
dark as origins
where the dead
can drift
unscathed . . .

and who will come
to confirm
the doing

who will testify

it is done

and who will say
the strike was made by them . . .

By water then
where great orange fish
pick
at eye
        or mouth
                or genital

where the corpse can settle
clean
and safe
white as any dream
born in your fetid air.

(After a performance by SOON 3, San Francisco, CA 1982)

Rasslin – a found poem

For Neil Lehrman

Jus in case I didn mention
I'm from Florida
home a the Seminole –
          mostly
bullshit & gators . . .

You drive the swamp – see big boards advertisin
the prime bouts
It's the fack
celebrates these parts –
Rasslin Gators

A one-time thrill – no shit
got dudes in town
walkin roun
in half their skin
beats cockfights n bullfights all t'hell . . .

Well, I'm gonna do this tune bout rasslin gators – cep
that alays minds me of another story bout
bein back home fur the cure
drugs & all that shit – I'm

in this center see
where this dude
jacks-off every morning bout 5 am
wakes the whole damn place
humpin & hollerin
like he's possessed
I swear t'Christ
He never even used his hands
Jus humped the goddamn bed
rubbin right through the sheets
like none a us was even there –

Now I don put down jackin off, fack
I wish we's all that free – no
it's that noise, all that thrashin round – almost like he's
pained ur scared – yeah – like – you got it – like rasslin
like rasslin gators

(After a performance by Sandy Bull May 20, 1976
San Francisco, CA)

October 9, 1967

For Che Guervara

Toads sing at sundown
Long, rhythmic chants
Like the clapping of shoes.

Hoot owls light the sky.
Roosters molt in the jack-pine
Turning blue.

I camp in the snail's track. Small
veiled girls serenade my night,
their soft bones turned
fodder for the goats.

The mountains are hardest
Trails like polished eyes.

I slake my thirst on the lips of tigers,
rest in the throats of hummingbirds.

In La Paz

I sell my teeth for beetle's wings, trade
radios for gunpowder,

20

assemble bombs.

I visit Beirut
400 Moslems shit & belch-up fisheyes,
in Terre Haute they crush my hands,
castrate the horse,
flog my mole till his asshole pops;
Dallas buries my tongue,
Hangs my skull in dormitory windows.

I keep to the backroads.
My eyes leave a slick trail on your bedroom doors.
Your plumbing's jammed with my clenched fist.
I'm under your collar
Burrowing along your spine.

Midwestern Christmas

The boy in the blue snowsuit is fat,
nearsighted and snivels
when the whip
snaps back
the snow.
His hands are fans:
bruised blue coral
humming
in the corners
of his elastic mittens.
He's mumbling to himself
stumbling in the slush
one foot in
one foot out.
At the pond
he stops,
cackles at the ducks
growing drunk in the ice.
He thinks
how big he will grow:
Big as the trucks
that haul the hogs away;
Big and bland
as these sloping plains

murmuring to themselves
their own private song.
So he slides along
the surface
of this frozen lake
taking stock – counting
the years ahead,
swallowing the days
one after another,
growing
and planning
his own secret home
under acres of this Midwestern snow.

I've Seen It Again

For Denny Zeitlin

your absolute hand
raking the tin leaves
of the little African
finger piano
while your other
strides the Steinway
toward some complete
harmonic feat.
And I distinctly hear your foot
stomping its own
accompaniment
as if it were
running in place
far ahead.

From

It's Mother's Day

1996

I Carry The Dead

I carry the dead child in my pack
with dried fish, my canteen
& a sealed tin of plums.

I carry his bloody shirt in my belt
his favorite toy
a pup he'd had since birth
over my shoulder
its eyes jiggle & snap
its stuffing leaks
it knocks against my ribs with every step.

I raised this child
from his mother's arms
washed his puckered skin
combed dust from his hair
picked crusted tears from under his eyes
pearls of shit that clung in strands to his stubby legs.

I bear this boy with a hunter's grace
careful to measure my stride
conserving breath
past men eating fire
past manicured lawns

past peddlers of teeth.

I take this stiff corpse
no more than one year old
to dig his grave beyond the trees
where his people grazed sheep
honed tools, married & birthed

under bows of flowers
where a stream may
at any moment
break through polished stone.

It's Mother's Day

and I've been watching 900 US Cavalry disembowel Chief Black Kettle's
Cheyenne women and their kids at Sand Creek, Colorado In 1864 cutting
out only the mature genitals to stretch on saddle knobs in Ric Burns'
documentary "The Way West".

It's Mother's Day and I've come back from a late lunch with mom after an
emergency trip to a Vet who put down our dying dog. She was an old
breeder who'd folded after her 2nd heart attack,3 litters and 5 years on the
dog show circuit.

Her handler called her Jubilee and gave her up to us to
nurse through her dotage.

She left us behind with a rambunctious pup she reared as
her own.
We'll all need to adjust.

Our friend Renee recently lost her dog of sixteen years.
Without her, she says, the walls don't square.
They'd crossed the continent together
DC to Illinois to California.

In Colorado, Fort Lyon,
where Chivington mounted his assault,
lies southeast of Pueblo
where my son's mother has a sister.
Arid in summer, brutal in winter,
not many settled here
on the way west.
Not many tourists.

Rooms rent cheap in southeastern Colorado
Food's generally fresh.
A good place to barter, shop for bowls,
scavenge artifacts.

A good place
on a long trek
to pull up
get mom a coke
let the kids stretch their legs and pee.

A good place too
for the family dog to cut loose and maybe dig for bones.

Jim Talks About Coyote Mask

For Jim Allen who owns the gift & knows its powers

I can't believe she'd want to give it up.

Bad vibes, she said. Too dark.
Or some such nonsense. I think power.

The dancer with the cunning tongue,
mesmerizing rattlers, toads & puma alike.

I picture him totally out of control
rabid

head wagging
frothing at the mouth

goatee flecked with spit
smacking his lips & licking his gums

terror waiting
out of reach

ready to snatch away
your kill.

No wonder Zuni
treasure tales of his treachery

why he's mascot to despair.

Bobbing and weaving he circles
all eyes follow.

He's been known to tease, to change his shape, disappear, appear again.

There are those who've seen him dining at the finest
 tables, blessed by the most elaborate churches.

My neighbor recounts the time in the desert
when she waited to be rescued from the cold & Coyote took her to his den

fed her a meal of free-range hen
then mounted her

turning loose a tantalizing truth she'd been forced to hide for years.

Power.
Did I say?

He holds the lever

turns it at his pleasure
singing

yip-yip-yip-a-we
YIP-YIP-YIP
CO - YO - TE!

Letter to Sophia

I should have known, even before the wind had shifted &
the stench of flesh on fire peeled sweat from walls, from the whistling in
my ears, the resonant whack of cracking spines, bodies rotting in the road.

I should have hocked my gun, torched my fatigues,
joined your neighbors for the long march out. Instead
& I tell you this with chalk in my mouth,

I drank with the rest, took my turn in the teenage girls,
forced the sons to do dog to their mothers, yes,
all this I did & more.

I should have known, when my beard turned white,
when men were forced to bite the balls from their brother when I prayed
for rain to wash semen, shit & tears to the sea,

you would never take me as I was, never kiss my eyelids with your tongue
as you did, never slip your cool hands under my shirt, press your cheek
against my naked back,
never again trust me to be clean

After Vukovar 1992

This Garden These Koi

for Josie and Denny Zeitlin

They've been with us for several years.
They eat from our hands.
They lift
their curved lips
(ever so slightly)
they suck our fingers.

We stretch out along the bank of the pond
dangling a free hand in the cool water.
With the other
we stroke each other's neck
occasionally
nibbling here and nibbling there.

This garden these Koi
hyacinth, lavender
mist in late afternoon
the simple rhythms of falling water.

This garden
these Koi
my hand along your back
your fingers in my mouth.

From

Barcelona Diary

2000

There's An Old Man At A Bus Stop

Boots buffed. Gray hair neatly dressed. Slacks formal &
pressed. He stares at nothing in particular . . . a spot in passing:

the lady & her poodle   coed with briefcase & helmet   the sun reflecting
passing traffic in the windows of Finca
Forcadell . . .

He's folded his arms across his chest but is not defiant
rather, content & lost for these few moments . . . to contemplate his
horizon through

clear brown eyes / content to wait for the proper bus that he knows will be
coming soon.

Exposicio Marc Chagall   @   Centre Cultural Caixa Catalunya

". . . To me, art is mainly about a condition of [my] soul" Marc Chagall

He's the horned goat in red robes with his Cheshire grin, the trout that swims above the marriage bed, a chicken chasing a Rabbi home.

He's the violin that plays the funeral, the cow that gives green milk, the clock that marks our time.

He's the husband & the wife adrift in midair, a Shofar trumpeting Rosh Hashanah, a loafing Hassid called to prayer.

He's a gambler with his foot in his mouth, a drunkard pissing against the fence, Jacob battling his angel.

He's Abraham with a knife at Isaac's throat, a lover stroking the skin of his beloved, Job frozen in despair.

He is, in fact, all that he has gleaned & pressed to his breast & wrestled to the earth & tamed & . . . reluctantly released . . .

Girona: 'The Call'

A capacious & commanding Star of David has been crafted at the center
of a courtyard in Girona's old city, just up the steps from Carrer de la
Forca,

in the district known as . . . "The Call' or . . . 'Jewish
Quarter,' &

although I listened for some echo of a cantor's lilting
chant & murmurs of those great debates which shaped the visions of
Kabbalah, today

there was only the clamor of gulls chasing the tide on the
Onyar & folks like us climbing stairs that join these resurrected rooms

that were the homes for hundreds in its day. &

while the ghosts of the Sephardim refuse to speak, there
is no doubt, at that crucial moment, they would come again & tap the
right man to make

a minyan for a bris or funeral or Friday prayers . . . ever
respectful of an

omniscient God / un-seen & un-attendant but . . . insistent & immaculate & for whom they must reiterate each day of their lives

the ritual of the cleansing & the binding of the word upon the hands & upon the eyes & all else that these teachings have fore-told.

Fundacio Antoni Tapies – Merce Cunningham: An Exhibition

"The dance is an art in space and time
The object of the dancer is to obliterate that." M C

I want to run into a wall & through it . . . climb to the moon on a rope of
the finest linen . . . I want red to bring love & magenta a rippling pine . . .
I want to ride on a cloud of spaghetti . . . swim through canyons filled with
hungry crocodiles . . . I'll be a bird chasing scorpions across the sand . . . an
Anaconda wrestling my weight in the shape of a fawn . . . I'm a galloping
Rhinoceros unchained & spinning to my freedom on The Milky Way . . . a
word looking for a sentence . . . a small boy on his way to second grade . . .

**

When you've turned the lights down low & are expecting your lover to come
toward you naked & willing . . . you'll have rain & a visit from your sinister
mother . . . While you gather your clothes for a trip to Paris you'll become
bored & lonely & eat your lamp & burn letters . . . If you have not
remembered where you lost your soul & whether it was important . . . you
will . . . How you manage does not matter – take that first time with the
clock & how it stopped just short . . .

**

I'll be the sun & the moon & the stars if you'll be the portrait & the door & our day-to-remember . . . I'll be the horse in the valley & the gentle rain & a river winding & a blossom about to fall if you'll be a parrot in flight, the rising tide, my moment-of-awareness . . . I'll be the last train to Mount Diablo if you'll be my locomotive . . . I'll be the bed . . . you be the sleep . . . I'll be the serpent . . . you be Eve . . . I'll want . . . & . . . I will . . . & . . . I can

   . . . & . . . I am . . . & you too

mothers & sons

She's a small woman who gestures vigorously & talks rapidly & wants him to know where she's been & the excitement of that time & how it will be this time & what they will see & he listens & tries to hold his eyes on hers & she occasionally hugs him & kisses his cheek & tells him how good it is after all these years & he responds with dinners & chocolate & tickets to a ballet & trips to the mountains & they walk arm in arm: 'comrades on the day' . . .

I've seen her before. Usually alone. But today . . . today, something is different . . . today, her hair has red highlights & she wears a new summer dress & today, she has her son on her arm &

he's careful to guide her down the museum walk & up the steps to the train to Tarragona & to the bus on Montjuic & up the hill to Montserrat & he orders the proper wine & insists he pay &

all this after a dark turn in the road & the distinct sound of shredded metal & an eerie silence that lasted months & she waited at the end no matter how long it took & now they walk arm in arm . . .

dos barrachos

The big one with the bloody eye belts the little one who runs away but the big one chases him waving his half empty bottle of cheap red wine & drags him back by the scruff of his neck like a chicken to be plucked & the little guy tries to sit quietly but the big one keeps railing at him & swatting his head for emphasis & someone goes for the cops who are in the station at the side of the plaza but they refuse to join in & merely watch from their little window & someone else tries to separate the two but the big one yells & spits & takes a swing at him & falls in the street where he belches & farts & when he can stand he digs out his limp dick from his stained jeans & tries to spray the crowd but instead pisses a short thin stream mostly down his leg & when he sees his partner has disappeared he starts off too with his open pants screaming at the top of his voice that we are all ass-holes & sons-of-bitches & no doubt some of us are & other choice Catalan insults that I cannot understand but some do & applaud & cheer & he turns & flicks his tongue & a dog barks at his heels & he tries to run but keeps tripping over his trouser cuffs & falls again & sits in his own dim light & stares off down the street & hangs his head & weeps.

storm

the skies breathe a deep sigh & timid dogs howl & bark & in the heart of the night young women from the city parade at their windows naked or in shimmering gowns to witness the great muttering from the north the inarticulate roar of he who is trapped in the clouds but reaches for their hand & shoots down as if on a thin white cord the ladder to climb.

coffee

We engage the first at ten AM. Not too powerful - smooth & sincere with a serious float of rugged cream.

At twelve there'll be another somewhat more complex & mature with a hint of cinnamon & devious strength.

 At lunch a third, delicate but brutal with a simply charming chocolate tart.

Our clandestine rendezvous at four is usually colossal but calm while five is likely to be demanding & regal & black.

At eight there's the rude & the mighty but ten's unusually brief, courteous & extremely courageous . . .

we've tried to avoid eleven (always barbarous & frank) but if we survive there's always twelve

with her smug & vulgar . . . & a hint of rage.

Fiesta Major de Barcelona: Gegants, Nans, Capgrossos & Bastoners

. . . fifteen feet these giant Kings & giant Queens led by a grinning cat & tracked by a pair of cocky birds whose all-too-human breasts elicit smiles & sighs & after them fishwives with plates of hake & roly-poly heads too big for their feet & barons & priests & sailors & kids to play the pipes & drums coursing down The Ramblas tossing confetti & streamers & dancers tumbling & twirling & hoisting their canes in stride & time to the bands which clamber & clang & whistle & clap & the giants too are spinning & the crowd surges & families race ahead to snap pictures & we all merge in the square to applaud & take a wine or coffee & sample cakes & handmade chocolate & honey & marmalade & soon drift up the street to the next plaza where a lone guitar & flute remind us of a quieter time & we drop a coin & listen & gather our strength for today's 'Fiesta' & there're many hours more to come.

in those days

There are women here, mature women, who ride the bus with dignity & a
delicate fan to compliment their silks & striking prints & some sport a cane
or hand-sewn umbrella or a clutch from Riera or Cartier to hold their
private needs for a trip to Sonia's for dinner or Dr. Font's for that sore tooth
or, Yes, an afternoon rendezvous in Guell Parc with a certain gentleman
from her youth who is widowed & . . . & while I watch she nonchalantly
opens her fan & begins, with her wrist cocked just so, to stir the air & with
it a sly smile seems to come or is it a hint of perspiration caught in the corner
of an eye that has made her turn this delicate rose or is it a memory or vision
of herself with her first fan at a cotillion or summer fiesta when she was a
girl in Tarragona & the young men would come to her mother & ask her to
walk with them & it was the fan that kept her engaged & wise to the talk
& time & whether the air had warmed or cooled & the name of the man
had changed & she was on her own as she was mostly in those days & could
do no wrong.

September 11

*In Fossar de les Moreres 'cemetery of the mulberry trees' lie the remains of those
who died during the siege of Barcelona in 1714 which ended the war of Spanish
Succession.*

. . . but the keepers laid the invaders beyond the trees &
only patriots to the center, so too the digger who found his son a traitor &
tossed him out as well.

Such is the lot of the soldier.

. . . but it's La Fiesta Nacional de Catalunya when the flag
is flown high & the anthem plays all day & the graveyard (paved now &
host to an eternal flame) swells
with memories of the old grave digger &

cheers for "Free Catalunya!!!" resound around the walls of
the church of Santa Maria del Mar & peddlers hawk
key-chains & pendants & pins &
the story of the siege is acted out & images exhumed &

we're tempted to raise our arms in salute & cheer &
whistle & march away with our banner raised
but we are the 'stranger' here & have no claim so
we step aside & only snap a picture & leave

down the quiet 'street of the whores' for a coffee & an
 early lunch but we wear our Catalan flag in our lapel &
nod to all who pass & smile & for a moment –
we too belong.

wine

Ellen & I usually take a break each afternoon, you know, a little breather
in the sun.

There's this quiet café just across from our pension & the wine, Ah . . . the
wine's sensational.

Jordi, he's the owner & our self-appointed guide to Barcelona, makes his
own

at his father's country house & stores the oldest here. A basic Tempranillo,

deep purple in the afternoon glow & a white, thinner than Chardonnay
but full of fruit & almost

perfectly balanced. Jordi says, "My wine is like a woman, over time, the
budding breasts &

spindly legs of adolescence, firm to curves & blossom like hibiscus in its
season." "Age." he says,

"That's the secret. We are used to that. Serrano hams my uncle hangs for
years, Mama's holiday Paella

she begins on Monday for a Sunday feast."   His café's just a block from a
Gaudi masterpiece,

Antonio Gaudi, whose 'Church of the Family' is still being built these
hundred years – Jordi says,

"When the last scaffold has been dismantled &
The masons have retired, it will be polished to perfection."

He urges, "Don't rush these days in Catalunya, savor its scent, its taste, its
rugged textures,

like the building of this monument, like the mandate of a marriage, we
must practice patience, ripen & mature,

like my wine in oak & in its time we'll come to draw a glass & toast our
luck!"

dog

*. . . good dogs & bad dogs, savvy dogs & bitter dogs, playful dogs & lazy dogs,
winsome dogs & mangy dogs / dogs which hunt & found dogs, dogs which cry &
lost dogs &*

lost dogs wander the streets with their tongues wagging from their hot
mouths looking & sniffing for that special friend they've missed or who
has missed them or who

left them for dead in the road after dark to wander for hours in search of
that connection, that familiar tie to their small world which has been lost or
stolen or misplaced, that

key to opening up their life which they cannot open on their own & to
which they are linked by years of trusting that hand to stroke an ear, offer
up a bone or a warm place

on a cool night when few are about & the hour is becoming late & no one
has stopped to say, "Here boy. Here girl. I'll take you. I know the way. It's
just up there . . ." & the dog will go on

into the next day & past that to the next & may never stop 'till the scent is
as lost as he & there is no more . . .

From

The Man With His Back To The Room

2 0 0 6

October 14, 2000

For Tom & Jennifer

Travelers on the wing & time to spare & a meal in store. "Fill Up Here" reads
the sign at Cafeteria José i Maria where we drop our duffels & portable gizmos
& relax over a plate of spinach & wild mushrooms & down a glass or two of
Torremilanos from Ribero del Duero & catch the eye of a painter from Santa
Monica who knows a haunt or two & offers coffee at his studio . . .

I've come to the gate & knocked three times & spread his ashes as he
asked &

I've planted sage & thyme & mint at the base of the fountain in the yard
& asked forgiveness &

I've been drenched in the rain of days on the road & learned to savor a
bitter tongue & lime &

I've listened to the ramblings of men at the altar who rub against each
other & kiss &

I've seen the women too who handle their sister's bodies like their own &
lick an ear & tongue &

I've weathered the coast in an open boat & fished for my dinner in coves
& gullies & killed &

now I ask to be left alone to steal a dream or two for myself & to hollow
out a small place under these fading stars.

A Dressing Gown

It may have once embraced the moist & perfumed skin of a Japanese
Geisha as she plucked the strings of her Samisen & sang praises to her
prince . . . It

may have served as the leisure robe of a dark-eyed Tahitian goddess as she
tempted the passions of a lusty sailor from Lisbon or Marseilles . . . Its
green

satin sheen may have once graced the long lean body of a fiery courtesan
from Barcelona or Paris or Marrakech &
who will know & who will come to tell.

Today it hangs in the privacy of my bedroom where my lover comes to
treat me to her unique & eager style of love &

when she lets it slip Oh so slowly from her shapely shoulders it colors my
dreams with its red & yellow peacocks & pheasants & soaring hawks &

as she straddles my mouth & treats my lips to her exposed sex I hear the
peacocks scream & feel the hawk's breath in my ear & it's then

I roll her on her back & ride into the night remembering the light &
tawny lovers of the earth & the dreams each has shared with each.

Marrakech

The Souks: day

The boy with fire in his eye & the quick hands of a thief shuttles us
beyond the chickens & lame donkeys
to see how wood is seduced from a block to a box & lacquered & inlaid
with silver & stone &

copper is twisted & bent & scored & etched & polished &

the tattooed hands of women & roasted dates which hum against the
gums & snakes that bite & monkeys & Iguanas that do not . . . &

mint tea & honey cakes & a single carpet sixty feet across &

deep in the interior on a darkened street we're led to the peddler of bones
who dances his fingers across a board shuttling skulls & knuckles & toes
down the alleys of my life which throb & narrow & glow . . .

Men. & the aroma of roasting meat & fish fried crisp & boiling pots of
broth & couscous piled high with diced tomatoes & rosted eggplant &
chicken & almonds & onions &

Men.   Eager & jostling & eyeing the foreign women who've come to see
& the air thickens & the air stiffens &

a dozen lanterns create pockets of light where young boys box for money
& musicians & singers & some stop for a meal & some for a sweet & the
menu is the same & the menu is different &

Men . . . call you to 'Come' & 'Sit' & 'Taste' & chanting & drumming &
you may be tossed from your place & whirled around or running

the dark streets where cars & carts converge & you cannot breathe &
cannot remove your mask but dance to the drum with your caftan stained
& beard askew & a thin chain that glistens on your neck & . . . Men . . .

Olives

'Plant trees for your children & the fruit will come for theirs…'

A young herder plays his flute & his leader her jangling bell & in the olive groves the trees are full & soon, before the ripest begin to fall, the women will come & spread the cloths & the young men will climb out where they can & shake the tree & loose the rest & rush to the press & that night the pungent oil

Green & black & gray & pink & purple & cracked & whole & pitted & stuffed &

cured with onions & garlic & peppers hot & peppers sweet & thyme & dill & tarragon &

sampled with breads from Barcelona & cheeses from Pamplona & a cool glass of Fino from Jerez &

the oil you'll drizzle on ripe tomatoes & onions & anchovies & toasted baguettes & this you'll serve in the shade

of a misty August afternoon as the families gather & the kids race to soccer & the women shuffle & riffle the cards &

grandfathers stare like pilots into the distance for that perfect place to land
. . .

Amputees

In Sierra Leone the intruders cut off her hands & his arms & her legs & they cut & left & in the chaos that is the hospital for the disabled all the appendages have escaped incineration & march or crawl or stutter or stagger like an army weathering winter but not in Sierra Leone . . . it is too hot in Sierra Leone . . . Here – they march like an army drenched in sweat & blood that leaks from their ruptured veins & they hunt in the bush & the back-streets & alleys for 'Junior' who did the cutting & wore his name plainly & with pride & his eyes glowed & his machete & he spoke mumbo-jumbo & preached freedom & peace & butchered & left this young girl, no more than fifteen years, to be fed & cleaned & used by the merciful or those who are not.

There's A Street with No Name In A City You've Painted Black

The arms that wave from the windows are black & the cats that roam the street are black & there are black beards & black hands & black market toys & you've blackened the windows & shut my eyes & locked my door & painted a black X on my back & when they come to claim their prize you feed them black bread & black beans & black rice & lift the black iron pan & toss your black mushrooms & black butter & when I reach out to make you stop you drown me in the black rain that falls from your thick red wound.

Confluence

For Dian & Judy

On the ride north we reminisce about family ties & kids on trial &
growing up estranged & how discovery can set us free &

where three rivers converge there's the constant & submissive sea to
welcome & absorb the sludge & sap of continents &

where the monument to Lewis & Clark celebrates challenge & risk we're
encouraged to contemplate transcendence & what it takes

to map mountains & lakes from the bow of a birchbark canoe & how the
yowl of a hungry Grisly pawing the air in spring might churn the blood &

how some men assume futility but insist on going on & when the time is
right, accept the Salmon's challenge & swim upstream to spawn & die.

Astoria, Oregon – November 29, 2002

She Wears A Scar

She wears a scar that curves from her lip across her cheek to her ear. She
was cut by a man who found her home &

when she smiles (which is rare) it rises like another mouth & puckers like
it would open & speak &

when she runs (which is often) her features tense & her new mouth glows
like a wire – hot & powerful &

she wears one glass eye on a thong around her neck to see in the dark & a
needle taped to her leg &

she flies a black flag with a man's face at its center & has etched a red scar
on its cheek & the number 6 between its eyes &

at the end of her street she's painted a door in the eight foot wall & when
she must, she opens it & runs through &

down the hill to the river & to the ship that carries her back to the
beginning.

The Woman in The Window

wears white & weeps blue tears down her thin cheeks & her silver hair is a
nest of chickadees &

around her neck from a silver chain a miniature black cage where a white
cricket lives &

in her heart there's a hole that has never been filled & in her mouth words
she will never speak but

chews them day by day until they are the color of white paste that will be
her meal for the night.

The woman in the window cannot find her way in the dark & depends on
the moon & the shadows it casts

to make a path for her to come & go & in the day she is motionless in her
chair of asphodel & weeds &

looks to the horizon like a queen waiting for her lost consort & when I see
her, as I often do, I wave &

she offers a rare smile & I see her teeth are strong & her eyes turn bright
as the darkest stars.

What We Will Not Know (of Torture)

When I first met Jamie & Beth they were swimming in the river Styx.
You know.
The one keeps us from walking round with the dead.
Well.
For a while.
Anyway.

It begins with grumbling
like the grinding of granite knobs
a hammering & battering of steel plates & the crack
of a whip & bones snapping or a slug to the jaw &

bombs & rifle fire &
the smothered bodies sliced &
diced & spit back between the iron ribs
that separate those behind the screen from the rest of us.

& the klieg lights come up & into your eyes to search the back of your
head for a brain unsprung.

& the knuckle-wrenching climb to the wire that's wired to the generator
that's wired to the dam that spikes

like heroin its electric charge to the veins.

& before the night begins again there's the unmistakable bitter-sweet
scent of shit & the rank stink of toasted flesh & the sweat of fear & . . .

& a hole is cut in the tongue of one young enough to be your grand-
daughter & a thin, barbed chain is dragged though that hole & her blood
is collected in an urn that's delivered to the priest that placed her here &
there's the smell of her roasting at the foot of the god-head that holds
success as a gift & failure as the exception.

& the one who the soldiers desire is forced into the room saved for that
purpose & when they've divided her between them often & as they please
she's tossed to the hogs that surround this place & . . .

& when it's quiet again there's the small, wet sound of whimpering & on
the screen an enlarged hand is displayed while one by one its nails are
extracted & a mouth where one by one teeth are or have been & . . .

a man tethered to a chain is dragged though the slime that is the blood of
his comrades &

a scissors is rammed up his ass & another & a cut is made & another &
one at a time & then by hundreds &

the cage is a door & the door is a cage & a wall & the gurney is wheeled
through the yard &

bodies are tossed in the pit & the drivers arrive & the drivers go & . . .

the kidnapped & the captured are led away to wait for the night & the
knife & the glare &

the wounded to crawl & the river to rise & the sirens to cease

& the mocking . . .
When I last saw Jamie & Beth they were floating in the river we all called Styx.
You know.
The one that's supposed to keep us from walking around with the dead &
deranged.
Well.
For as long as we're willing.
Anyway.

After: Herrumbre (Rust) – Compania Nacional de Danza – Nacho Duato: Coreografia
Body and Cosmos: The Sculptural Art of Pre-Columbian Mexico – The Rituals

Out of The Dark

I speak of that place where a mystery will not be solved, where the suspects
speak in tongues & cannot look each other in the eye,

where the deck is always stacked against the players & no one to catch the
fallen.

I speak of a rendezvous with the hanged man who suggests a shovel & the
guard who demands retribution for night sweats &

will suck the last breath from those who were sent for help but
disappeared in a bottle.

I speak of Baby Huey & Charley D. lost on the last step of the last
landing, eyes rolled back, the needle stuck & dangling.

I speak for Ellen dead of her own hand, the 38 still cushioned in her
collapsed lap.

I speak out of the dark where light is only contrast: the outline of times
past, a hint of a future that could or may be. I speak

from the place that stirs a thousand pleas: for a door, a tunnel, a stick of
bone to lift the rock,

any thing or any way to stop the drumming in the ears, the stuttering hands, to finally escape the blinded mind.

In Memoriam: Richard Avedon – October 1, 2004

In The American West 1979-1984

This is not the American West of John Wayne or Warner brothers. No! This is the Amerika of John Lynch & Count Dracul . . . of Richard Avedon: This moneyed wise-guy who's come to snap the simple folks on the plains . . . to make an irritating image – How did he survive their rage? I guess we'll never know for sure?!

Eyes. You fix on the eyes: Black faced coal miners who stare down his lens. Their whites the only reflected light.

Beads of black sweat on a furrowed face in Eagle Pass, Texas / slick & sticky blotched skin of Oklahoma Oil.

White / Scaled / Gesso miners / Cody, Wyoming.

These images, too reticent to speak, squint or smirk or curse / Are mute / Are mutant / Are – at war with Avedon: Accuse – Suspect – Accuse.

They've been conned before / maybe by the best / maybe by his 'Clarence Lippard' drifter Sparks, Nevada,

by the playful nonchalance of 'Carl Hoefert' card sharp, Reno, Nevada or maybe they've been plagued by Syphilis or Gonorrhea in Salmon, Idaho or

lost their teeth in Albuquerque, New Mexico or / been scorched by
radiation in Rocky Ford, CO.

These men & women are not the talk' of cocktails or stuffed quail in New
York City – No! But, we agree, this is Avedon's country too, <u>Damn You!</u>

& when, like a ripe egg, these Great Plains part, the dead will carry the
living into battle & on each front you'll see their eyes first:

vacant & white & running blood.

Richard Avedon: Photographic Portraits – Caxia Forum: Fundacio "La Caxia"

This Is a Story Someone Is Trying to Remember

If I can,

I will tell you of the deer dying in the yard & starved pullets that wander
in circles in the snow &

how I need to find the place they scattered my father's bones & to hear my
mother's final words.

If I ever can,

I will tell you again of my need to caress my first wife & not be thinking,
'Would Gloria take me back as I was.'

When I remember,

I might tell you volumes of lies that disguise faces & florid afternoons with
wine & sesame cakes & visits from . . . but

chances are slim & the train will leave soon & before I go I wish you well
&

warn you of the blizzard that will come in the night (as it will) & the
family that eroded as some do &

the marriage that was doomed & the evil that kids do to one another &

if you remember to tell this story as it was told,

I will send you a letter with a number & a key & when you find what you
are looking for

maybe you will remember me.

Death & Contemplation

Cimetiere du Pere Lachaise – Paris, France – July 5, 2005

Lilacs, lichen, the stiff residue of a fallen egg / how cold the stone against a thigh

With official map in hand, they track the wake of the curious, the hunters
of families & those who've
come to pay homage

to their mentors whose unique lives composed a distinct allure: Frederick
/ Marcel / Edith / Gertrude / Oscar

Unrehearsed they're startled to find themselves lost in a reverential state &
even speak in whispers.
*

In the upper garden there're tributes to the Free French partisans &
tributes to the outcasts of Buchenwald, Dachau & Auschwitz:

sculptures of exhausted bodies, iron bones stripped of skin that speak of
the waste & carnage they saw before they fell.

& these two, alone inside their precious skins, shudder under this guise of
evil & resolve to honor the implied demand: "Never Forget."

Muscles tense & a bite at the back of the throat, they face their ride home together but apart

this is the day she tells him she will go on alone.

At War *[An Investigation]*

In times of peace the sons will bury their fathers.
In times of war fathers bury their sons.
Thucydides

A young boy has rummaged for scraps of wood & nailed them to
approximate the shape of an AK 47.

His (soon-to-be army issue) web-belt,
a single string he's slung across his back,

will have to do (as the love song says)
until the real thing comes along.

**

There's a farmer wandering the roads of Rwanda with four bent scythes
stretched across his back:

Death in an old disguise?

Maybe just another scavenger plying his trade?

**

Cahoots & chortling recruits parade / a pole / they've strung with the heads, hearts & testicles of the fallen.

As the maimed try to rise they flail & collide – It's then the Minotaur comes, sniffs the air & finding blood, feasts on the remains:

no bodies left to rot, no bones to store. No relics to hang on your slim altars.

**

The photographers that survive are always suspect:

"Where were you when he was shot?" "Where were you when the tanks rolled in?"

"   Where were you when she was shattered by the mines?" " Where .
. .?"

 "Where – Indeed."
Here – In the trench.

In the trench we've scooped from sand & broken plates,

where we've been trapped in a rain of blood & shredded skin, once a leg & even arms & when we can, we run with the stench & the stuff that clings & my film & . . .

**

If not me then who?

Who will bury this desiccated corpse / already a meal for the buzzards that
hover here?

The joke that passes says, "If you steal from these well-meaning janitors
you will be the first to be swept up in your next life."

I'm inclined to pass & walk away . . . & yet,
why not these birds?   I mean . . . why not . . .

**

In the end / there is always / memory

The red color of the flag that hangs on death's wagon or drapes the box
where Jamie sleeps

is the last your country-men & women will ever know of the blood that
was spilled here.

80

History is packed with irony & contradiction. Don't expect sustenance.

Rather, a snack to oblige & send you blithely on you way.

Never.

Look back.

The cabinet is empty / There's nothing left to claim.

**

Each drop that falls in the attendant bucket anticipates another soldier
down.

No matter.

There are always more buckets & more bodies to be tossed.

& if it's one drop at a time /

        one drop at a time it shall be.

So, it is said, by the shaman & the priests

who relish the last corpse / as if it were truly the body of hope brought
here to be resurrected

or not.

From

Intimacies

2 0 0 6

She's Chosen

She's chosen the middle of the road to make her stand: There's blood in her good eye & a bouquet of wilting carnations she waves like a flag above her head & chants her gibberish with a hint of longing & a tear or two & no one comes to reassure her or take her home or a cop with a badge & they honk her to one side & to the other & she bangs her flowers against their windows & curses their mothers & fathers & all their born & unborn & lifts her skirt & pisses against the door of the one that's stopped & I see a man at the corner who watches but doesn't move or seem to care until he comes into the light & takes her arm & holds her against him & rubs her back with his free hand & several applaud & continue on but when I turn she slaps him hard & wailing waves her broken bouquet & turns down an alley & snarls & whines & dares him to follow into the dark.

As Our Train Passes

As our train passes through the valley the men huddle at the windows to watch the women dance in the waning light. As the train picks up speed they dance faster, some run alongside, one lifts her breast to be kissed, another lies down in the grass & spreads her body wide for he who has the nerve to come into her. The train passes onto a red plain where a town once stood & relics still burn & there's a lone black horse & a wolf with green eyes & a boy with a whip & we're in the canyon & half-way across & the bells begin & we hold ours ears (as we've been told) but they pry their way inside & there's the clawing of the cat (as we've been told) & we reach for our lover's hand & look into her eyes & wait for the wind that's been promised & the patiently evasive moon . . .

It Came in The Afternoon Mail

It came in the afternoon mail. There was the picture just as he'd promised but it wasn't quite right . . . as she remembered there was a bamboo forest on the right & the sea on the left & there were no children playing in the foreground & she looked again & they are holding hands & looking at the camera but there had been a wire fence between them & a mountain behind & some scruffy kids were toying with a knife & that night she set the picture beside her bed & in the dark a faint glow seemed to emanate from the picture & there was a song – Yes, 'Yesterday' playing in the background & later, when she got up to relieve herself, the man in the picture began to talk & she heard him say, "It appears, I will not be allowed to see you again but I will always remember that other time & how we were & I wanted you to be with me for this last journey & although it is necessary that we part – I will keep the other picture & remind myself from time to time . . ."

From

After Goya

2 0 0 7

On his knees the lone man begs to be led away.

His wide white eyes stare into a sky all mottled & black.

He knows the future holds no salvation in the swirl of gas & scarlet rain

Spitting blood but still with his knife he rushes the guns & gunners oblige
with bayonets & shot as they've done to the dead & dying scattered below
& beyond.

The ax-man hacks at belly & bone – his partner straddles another driving
his blade deep & down that grizzled neck.

& now . . . The Women roil in rage w/thrust of sword or pike or the
heaving of stone – they joust & claw & bite, gouge eyes from the skulls of
the fallen.

Before rot / before buzzards / before the maggots bloom / scavengers haul
your dignity away / leave you stripped & bare. Who you were is
insignificant: you are the naked & the dead.

The women who've been kept to satisfy the troops are useless on the march. "There's no more time," says one officer. "No more time to fuck around boys. Do what must be done. There are more down the road."

"We should treat them here?" "There's no time. Leave them for Jose or Juan." "She's bleeding from the rectum." "Leave them. There's no time" "He's cut to the bowel. I'm thinking peritonitis." "No! No time . . ."

From

Escapades

2 0 0 7

After Her Suicide

he gave his first prostitute a Tag Heuer watch for a blowjob & the next a
puppy for the works & after a few more days of terror bought a ticket to
Katmandu & borrowed a fellow passenger's identity allowing him to enter
a dream of self-immolation from which he escaped; his skin the color of rust
/ missing his eyebrows, ears & right eye. When they found him wandering
the hills above Florence he showed them how he could remove what was
left of his head & replace it with another that resembled that of Orion The
Hunter – in his hands the corpse of The Lizard God & in his mouth a
tongue that could never again shape his defense or tell the truth.

The Winter

of his eighteenth year saw him wrestling alligators in Florida where he'd
gone to rescue his sister from opium & bad whiskey & eventually settled for
a role as Satan in the local production of JB where he won the Golden
Feather & a trip to Dallas where the real JB lived with his broken promises
& a wife who cooked roadkill & smoked cornsilk & often recited the entire
chapter of Revelations from memory like her mother & grandmother before
her & now to him who played his part well with tail & horns / fouled breath
& forked tongue that darted in & out between her pursed lips as he'd been
taught.

From

Improvisations

[The Chapbook]

2 0 0 7

After: *'Where's the entrance' No Stars Please*

Music by The Trummerflora Collective

She circled the edge & found herself slipping back to the day before last when she first noticed her skin was a thin shade of green & her eyes a hint of red & her father's voice from somewhere over the fence & when she looked a yellow dog stood to greet her & a blue lizard & she can hear a rustling under the stairs & two men on a tandem bicycle riding away & she follows with her drum & tambourine & bucket of coiled snakes & she whispers in the dark to whomever will listen, "I am Eloise & I have a secret" & once in a while a face will appear on the side of a building or in a window or in the sky & once in a while a broad-winged bird will dance toward her hopping from one foot to the other & pecking at stones & a voice may say, "You don't belong here" or "Watch where you step" or "Why have you come?" & with the thunder comes the rain & a crowd gathers in the culvert & someone is playing jacks with their daughter & another plucks a violin with one good string & she gnaws at her fingers & she will not stop.

After: *The Whisper Chipper 'Creative Music'* By Marcelo
Radulovich & Marco Fernandes

1

Humming from the gorge . . . an engine ignites the air – like a confluence
of ghosts & now . . . coyotes sing in the weeds & . . . you'll listen

for the light step of the dancer as she climbs & leaps & the collapsing trees
– the flock of Asian pheasants all red & green & yellow & blue &

his engine comes to crush all in his path & smoke & hand in hand the
couples climb the hill toward the monastery . . .

2

Swallows descend. The grinder shreds.
Julia runs ahead with her arms raised in surrender / a white flag in her
teeth.

They come quick now . . . to finish what they've begun.
Someone is playing a harp & when the water rolls over them . . .

a plea for salvation.

3

Our dinner waits in the field chewing its cud. Don't cry darling,
don't let them
    see you cry.

4

We're on the road with our belts tightened & no one to hear what we'll
say. This is the time to tell a truth you've hidden all these years.
This is the last chance for mock expression.
These are days of fire & milk.
Don't look back.

5

Come.
Let me hold your pale face.
Your lips on mine.

Your wish is my dream.

See the stars descending?
The night turns black with a yellow streak in its hair.

Button up. A sharp wind is rising. There'll be a storm from the east &
turbulence & rain & some will die & of course some will . . . die.

After: '*Punch press pull*' *No Stars Please*

Music by The Trummerflora Collective

Can you remember that first drum, the one with the metal rim & those sticks with their cotton knobs & how you proudly marched around the living room & the freight train that whistled by at precisely four thirty every Tuesday & Julie's eyes that were alternately blue & green & how she taunted you across the fence & her dog Buckskin who howled into the night & running home to mom with a broken tooth & no one home & blood in your mouth & the long climb to the roof where he was hammering away at his homemade boat & Jeremiah practicing his saxophone & the sun heating the tar to soup & the time Andrea fell through the skylight & had to be stitched quickly & butterflies on the milkweed & the sheriff coming after you with a warrant & everyone staring & pointing their fingers & how you left town & hitchhiked to Canada & the waitress who thought you were from California & offered her bed & stole the money from your boot & the last day of July when you won sixty on the slots & caught the bus that crashed in Detroit & the war games with live ammo & a jazz band on a flatbed & the B & O that ran all the way home & no one there to meet you except a guy playing bongos on a bench & a small girl asleep in his l

From

Homage To A Widow

2 0 0 8

The Widow Welcomes Her Lover

She's cooked his favorite: a coq-a-vin with fresh morels it being spring &
she alone.

He's cautious not to go too fast while she appropriately defends against
pleasure.

They are both keenly aware of the history that surrounds them in this
marriage bed

inhabited now by their urgency & passion – who will be the first to break
the bond –

how are they to survive?

The Widow Wanders into The Sea

There are jellyfish to consider, spiny urchins & the dreaded barracuda.

She never hesitates.

There were nights & days where a bong filled with marijuana settled her nerves.

& days when his being thrilled at a sunrise so radiant & warm as they are in the tropics

overcame the certitude of death at work – their days were measured one toke at a time.

From

It's Only TV

2 0 1 2

Letting Go

Normal is a stormy engine quivering in the background, a backfiring
Dodge Ram grunting up the hill toward your old man's house.

The sun's obscured behind burlap & buildings loose from their tethers,
tankers hauling bad water, your last image lifted for evidence.

Our neighbors reel from the hint of blood while Zampano, our old
malamute, flops despondent on the daybed.

Not totally unexpected it's come to this, time again to pack the truck, haul
out the old canvas bags, box-up snapshots & history &

turn from the sea to the mountains . . . to the place where the ghosts of
renegades & rustlers sleep with the ancestors of Geronimo & Cochise,
where

the summer sun filters through the morning mist & Siberian Elms, where
coyote, deer & eagles still breathe free, where,

for the eighth time in as many years, I'll try to find a place, light up the
logs, pour a glass, open these weathered books & begin.

Her Scar

lit up the night like a hot tongue licking across her belly.
She could hear the eighteen-wheelers cursing the ruts above the Hudson.

In November she'd resolved to bury his sword & pistol, leave the myth of
the hurricane behind, to oblige the wrestler.

That was then. This is now. Her scar reminds her of revenge. The boy
who came to the door last night left a bad taste.

She washed it away with Boodles & tonic, scrubbed the skin raw. What
was she thinking?   There's that kissing cat again.

Before the avalanche, before the whiskey rebellion, before monotony there
were the races & dress-up with high hats & roses.

Every time she came around they'd tell lies about that time – that time she
was whole, not like the broken banker who was her father.

Today began with steamed eggs, tomatoes & a nasty sore throat. If only
the nights were not impossible. If only nature could be trusted.

The Woman Who Sleeps with The Devil

rises after midnight, smokes a thin cheroot & lines her eyes with the blood
of his defiant guests.

She grows orchids in her greenhouse, distills rye whiskey & harvests the
neighbor's cats for stew.

The woman who sleeps with the devil never travels far from home, refuses
invitations & paints her windows black.

She will not speak of her past but hints at a rendezvous with an aunt who
guards the family bible &

brings her souvenirs: a rabbit's foot her father cured, her mother's ashes in
a blue porcelain urn, a tape of her sister's last words.

In winter, when his furnace heats their home, she spins wool to yarn &
weaves his exotic capes & shrouds.

The woman who sleeps with the devil has learned to identify renegades,
shanghai slavers, generals & executioners.

She's combed our streets for charlatans, those who sell the trinkets of god's
army to unsuspecting tourists.

They're a team, last seen wandering our fields hand in hand, she with a shovel & he with his torch & hook.

No one dares climb the hill to their rooms. We suspect anarchy & treason but will never interfere. Their privacy is our salvation.

The Man Waits

where dark water streams down rusted walls & the odor of death taints the air.

He cradles his small bindle of clothes, his unfinished manuscript, dinner in a paper bag.

She's been gone a month & he bites his lips thinking of his pathetic gestures – clasping her close those last nights.

Where was he when she needed to talk of the dark stranger in her dream or the horse that ran with her & would not stop?

Where was he when she called his name & heard (only) the echo of her own voice through their empty rooms?

The juice of their life together, like the steady drip from a cracked pipe, urged repair. There were times

they'd tried, much like the kiss before the storm, when mourning will not bring back what's been lost.

Today, as he lifts his eyes to scan the fading light he sees her, once again, walking away,

ensconced in her blood-red shroud, permanently
out of reach.

The Feather & The Rock

In this dream he's surrounded by a pack of yowling dogs & no one responds to his
calls. The hills move closer. A thick & steady rain . . . The clap & swish of wings

It's been like this,

night after night, a subtle devouring of spirit, a fever that grows more
fierce each hour . . . & these visions from his past:

his brother running up a hill into a rain of fire, a pen of pigs gorge on the
body of a goat, a butcher's knife

in the hands of a kid with no eyes, an angry snake coiled around its clutch
of eggs, his son's name on a head-stone written in blood.

It wasn't always.

There were seven years of plenty when his celebrated paintings captured
the angst & horror of the war & seven years of sorrow from which

he keeps an uncut rock of lapis to remind him of the dark blue nights of
the summers in the Morocco of his youth, a golden

pheasant's feather to remind him of the glow & texture of your smooth,
tan skin on the beach in Tangier the day you said goodbye.

The Woman Aaron

speaks of deserts: of oases & life, of honey dates & oranges, of quicksand
& hunters on horseback. The desert is like that,

life in one hand, death in the other. It's been so since the first camel, the
first scorpion, the first enigmatic nomad.

She also speaks of hyenas (driven mad by memories), of tanks &
phosphorus bombs & burns that never heal,

of missiles & mortars & vultures hunkering. Today is day eighteen of
desert war, war that began forty years ago, or

five thousand seven hundred sixty nine years ago. It cloaks the land of
milk & honey in its quilt of blood.

She speaks now of the fearful (huddled in shattered doorways) & the
broken (missing eyes & arms), the demented

(mumbling under blankets of bones) & of the heroic (clawing though
rubble seeking the lost, the dying & the dead).

Gaza Israel 1-13-2009

The Part of The Gypsy Girl

will be played by her twin, the one with one brown eye & one blue. She'll carry a guitar & dress in a velvet coat. Her smile will be painted green, her frown a pale pink. When she enters the secret room there'll be men with drawn swords & automatic pistols to guard her every move. & where she walks there'll be corpses to name & caskets she must number & bless. & when she's ensconced in the limousine she must not be tempted to kiss the general who sits at her right or the queen who sits on her left. & when they arrive at their inevitable stop she'll be carried to her room where they'll extract her eyes & replace them with the eyes of the goat who oversees war. It's then she'll be led to the edge of town where she'll be left to roam our valleys & mountains & sing of all she has seen.

The Resting Boxer

He poses on a rock apparently after a bout, elbows at rest on his knees, hands clasped, body & mind at ease after combat. He is naked except for a thong to protect his genitals. With broad shoulders & long limbs, a powerful chest & well-trimmed beard he has the bearing of a mature athletic man. A slight layer of fat at the waist hints at his aging. His swollen ears, right eye, nose & mouth tell of his beatings as does his bloody mustache & the drops of blood that have fallen on his right arm & leg.

She calls him *Atlas* after the god who led the Titans against Zeus & sketches him hauling the world on his back as the story tells. &

she dreams him in her bed where she bathes his broken face with kisses & his tortured body with her tears.

They've been lovers in another place – at another time, she's convinced & draws their coupling in charcoal & magenta.

Tonight she'll wait for him under the stars where he'd found her that first time, or so she remembers.

And because it was cold with wind & rain he'd wrapped her in his greatcoat & promised to calm the night.

From one season to the next & from wherever he was sent he would write
or call, or so she remembers.

Solitary & brooding he cannot think to fulfill her expectations or those of
his long-past youth.

Instead, he muses on the night's gambit where survival is the measure &
failure must be held at bay.

If they are a mated pair, as she would have it, they must belie all odds:
scatter roses if he's crowned – lilies if not.

The Resting Boxer From: Museo Nazionale Romano – Palazzo Massimo: Rome Italy

At The End

I turn to the beginning. That time when possibilities clawed at our skin
leaving welts like furrows where we could plant anything:

cotton, for the sheets on which we spread our bodies for hours of love &
sometimes just sex for the sake of the act itself,

tobacco, for those late-night sessions under the stars with brandy & coffee
& talk of revolution & mayhem & visions of traveling on,

apples, for the fallow days of winter when neither you nor I spoke of the
future or the past but were stuck wrestling with the descending cold,

spinach, for the salad to rival all salads with tuna & capers, Gorgonzola &
almonds, currants & pinoles, lime juice & cold pressed olive oil,

tomatoes, red & yellow, large & small to suck on a hot June afternoon at
the edge of a still lake where we'd dangle our bare legs & dream,

garlic, to heal the wounds we have & will inflict, not only those that run
red but those that are too deep to surface willingly,

sweet peaches, for the last days of August when we lay on luscious beds of
new mown grass & licked the juice that dripped from our sated lips,

&. . . gardenias, your mother's favorite, filling the house with their excess

– one in your hair that afternoon the ship arrived to carry you away.

From

Improvisations – Poetic Impressions From Contemporary Music

2 0 1 6

After John Adams' *'Gnarly Buttons'*

The Perilous Shore

The walls move: undulate in afternoon light. The final days are worth investigation. There's a hint of a dream in the melody – a hint of mourning, as tender as buttons on the back of a young girl's blouse. On the stage the ghost of Benny Goodman playing Mozart with the flare of a marching band & here they come down the road harmony up front up the steps & into the building where all scores are settled & payment made & from the window a glimpse of sea & a dream of water rising over the wall over the town over the countryside & the young boy runs to find his father & there's no one to tell & no one to remind him there is no use – it's over don't you know, don't you remember? It's then he picks up his clarinet & marches to his own drummer into town where the hip-cats play & dinner is served before the show & someone passes him a joint & it's Sunday & church bells & grandpa whips the old horse up the hill to the barn & he can feel the earth shudder & shake & here's dad in his Sunday best leading the romp & stomp into the park where the troll lives under the bridge with his ten kids & a sly dog named buttons & a grey squirrel named Phoebe . . . Is it too late to say goodbye?

After *'From The Waist Up'* <u>No Stars Please</u>

Music by The Trummerflora Collective

After scrambling for the last breath after chasing the last fix after wailing at the wailing wall after the big man threw the first punch after the small dark girl began to cry after all the money was gone after stumbling through the park after vomit & blood in the eye after the car left the station after crawling through snow after sleeping under the porch after the cat shit on your head after birdcalls & catcalls & sirens & cops after pistols & whips after no witnesses after a star fell after you missed my call after I sent flowers after you missed my call after I took another drink & another & after the bottle came the hovering in the calming sea after swimming into the sun after all.

After Terry Riley's ‘*Cadenza On The Night Plain*’

G Song

It's the song she sings in his ear as he strokes her tender bristles, licks the nipple that grows taut & dark under his kiss. & as he reaches into her to find that elusive spot she gasps as if to say Yes, you've found your way & his touch heats & her breath stiffens & his fingers & her lips & soon the stroke is urgent & her body reaches up to meet him & opens for him & she chants in tongues that reach back to the beginning, to the first man & the first woman, when it was new & sometime, even now, new again, or does it matter & Yes, it matters – Theirs is a tortured history – Stained sheets at the window – The right of the Patron – Even now – A play where roles are exchanged, where no holds are barred – Touching & biting excites. It may be hours or only a moment until it comes again: refreshed, startled, ferocious & untamed . . . It is the same each & every time – as they've come to expect & each & every time it is different . . . as they've come to expect.

After Jason Robinson's '*Tiresian Symmetry*'

7

You say, the future lies buried in the past, that only the blind one in the well can tell. & here the line begins: a sailor home from the sea, a king about to lose his throne, the crone with one good eye, supplicants & maidens alike, they all come. Remember me to your mother, he whispers. Out of the sea & into the mountains. Decade after decade. There's no escape. The pleasure you receive from a man's body is your right. Men are such empty vessels. Here, sweep me up in your big strong arms, take me to the top & remember, you were born to heal the sick of heart, those degraded by love, the tortured & the torturer. One man's curse is another's salvation. How many years has it been? Have you not had enough O wise one? & here the tale turns dark. There's a hole in the scrim through which the witches wander, one with a bloodshot eye, the other on her knees in pain. It's plain to see – if you can – if you ever can - again. The punch line is coming soon. You must learn to trust history. Hear them, hear the mumblers & the fumblers. They follow you like starved cows. It's your story. Tell it now . . . & tell it well.

After *'Third Time' <u>No Stars Please</u>*

Music by The Trummerflora Collective & the Sculpture of Tanya Story

Mourning doves & the hard striking nails of a Wolverine.
A whistle & the last drops of an early rain.

She's built a black virgin from foam & plastic & bone & she's opened its face

Follow the river. Hold close to the fence.

When did we last eat? Monday? Yes. Monday, I think it was Monday.

They've cleared the room & left the sheets of hot metal to rust.

They've welded a face to the wall & took turns with a razor.

she's planted a dog's skull at one breast & a seed pod in its slick vagina

I can see the body curled in the corner.
It's through the screen I'm looking.

she's skinned the head of an ox & raised it on wire & wings

As the day grows dark, a crowd begins to gather at the edge of the field.

One has a drum & another the leg of a goat.

Have you seen Hazel with her silver gown her silver turban her silver teeth?

Will you sit at my left & read to me from the golden book?

& she's split the naked torso of her twin & trimmed its fissures with ink & poison quills

The rain has begun again. Helicopters circling in pairs, a mastiff & a red Ferrari.

First, they were arranged in a line & then one at a time they were led away & after a while no one was left.

While Listening To Mingus In The Rain

Thunder. Counting beats. Her red lips. The barking dog. Simonize. Who
will clear the airways? Who will unload the heroin & baby formula?

A bucket of chicken. Two Taiko drummers. Alabaster. The Ides of
March. Ripe bananas. Cappuccino. Chloroform.

At the end of the house someone is playing a fiddle out of tune & another
is about to collapse as his blood pressure drops precipitously.

A monkey with a cold. Mother's milk. Anagrams. Evidence of an erection
after years of impotency. Bluetooth. Smog. Scars.

Tattoos. The Day The Earth Stood Still. Harmony. A kid's locomotive.
April afternoons. Home away from home.

Has love been too hard? How about a one-night-stand with the person of
your choice? Someone who reminds you of your sister? Or . . .?
Creamed corn. Octopus. Rambling Jack Elliot. Darwin. A god without
heaven. Smoking Monte Christos on Christmas Eve.

As they prepare for bed he rubs a little salve on her clitoris with the
promise it will double her excitement. He was right.

Napkins. Nephews. Oil of Mulberry. Teachers with agendas. A smoking gun. Blood on the sun. Marlborough Man on fire.

Take two at bedtime. Stroke the cat. Mustard. It's a long way from here to there. Wish for a trumpet. Swing upon a star.

The last lap. Santa Claus. Irony. In the back of bus number thirty-nine under seat fifty-two you'll find your mother's maidenhead.

Bye-Bye Blackbird. Kiss me again. The way you did in the movies. Don't you remember? Saturday afternoons? We were fourteen.

The Herbie Mann Trio at The Stage. Iona's pussy. Her brother's right hook. Lunch time on 63rd St. Who knew?

An argument with the devil. Cold Turkey. Marshaling martial arts. Out of respect. This is no honeymoon. Where are the orchids?

When the goat mounted the sheep . . . Havoc. Holsteins on the run. Your aunt comes to stay & brings Oscar the Parrot.

One by One. She lights his fire. Order out. Take what comes your way & don't act so surprised. Jack of hearts.

Robbing Peter to pay for the cocaine. In the wings. After the fact. Before the mast. & so it goes. One bad joke after another. Rhubarb.

She unceremoniously unzipped his pants & lifting his hardening cock leaned forward & began to suck it. Sunrise at six forty-five / sunset at eight fifteen.

Quarter horse. Gatling gun. Amelia Earhart. The disquiet that follows. Amnesia. A better tomorrow. Orange drapes. Cousins.

It takes two. What can you offer? I bet the farm. Carry me back to old Virginny. Tienes para mi un beso negro?

Ripe balloons. Torment. Sale this Saturday. Thirty-five laps to the mile. Third place at thirty-seven. Not bad. Sequoia.

A trunk full of monkeys. Uncle Mike always made time. Stamps from the Saar. Hitler's mustache. Six million Jews. Poverty.

I sit by the window & watch the rain. I sit by the window & drink my wine. I sit by the window & remember Chicago & Miles . . . &

I remember Denny roiling the keys at the Am-Vet's hall in Champagne-Urbana, butterflies & that foxy Cordelia in the closet.

Marble & car horns. Amputees & Sri Lanka. My mother's ample breasts. My Father's judgments. Arial bombardment. Quest.

Sundown. Arrested wind. Time for a walk in the forest. Remove your gloves. There's sure to be chanterelles &, if we're lucky, morels too.

Taos, NM 7/26/09

After Miles Davis' *'Bitches Brew'*

Miles Runs The Voodoo Down

Drink. Drink. From the common cup. Hear her. The one who comes. Through the mirror. To enchant. You. Drink. & smoke. You are a mirage. A mystery. To be buried. A confusion. Manacled. Set upon. By demons. In the stew. Drink. They will come soon. To harvest. What. Is left. Never. Leave her. In charge. It's always been. This way. Don't / you / know. The last left. With the goodies. Stir the pot. Toss in all you've brought. Be clean. It takes more. Than willingness. You / tell / us. Speak. As you always have. I'm the one. I've always been. The one. She whispers in his ear. Makes him shiver. Nips his neck with her forked tongue. Teeth. Her magic goes. Further. He. Follows. Makes up his mind. She takes it / oils it. Sparks leap from her eyes. Flames from her fingertips. She's naked now. Her glossy mound. Her sagging breasts. Sagging skin. She. Transforms to a goat — horns & hooves & just as quick – back. To woman. Young. Firm & . . . Voluptuous. Curls her finger. Motions him. To follow. Her fine high ass / so round, so muscular. He follows. Hungry. You bet. Horny. For sure. Afraid. Not any more. She's made. Her point. Points him. Toward. Chance. Survival. Maybe that too. The room swims in smoke. It's raining. Someone. Passes a cup & / we drink. The room slows. The rain washes. Over us. She's back. For the next. There'll only be a next. You can count on it. There's always. Next. The rain stops. She's dressed. A bright red gown. Twirls. Her ripe. Hips. The walls hum. With. Every. Thrust. Pipe. The Piper. Pipes. It's Fast. It's Urgent. It enthralls. Entrances. Captivates. It's meant to threaten. Get down. On the floor. On. All fours. She'll have her way with you. Now.

After Elliott Carter's *String Quartets*

No. 2

She wore silver slippers & smoked a thin black cigar. He walked around her observing each flourish, every tick. She would be his study for the afternoon. It was a museum after all. He remained outwardly calm when she slapped his face. She had a spider monkey on a leash & ground the cigar butt under her thin heel. It was Thursday. Not very crowded. The next time they met she kissed him on the lips & promised hours of pleasure. That was in December. There's a chill in the air. As they walk a blue sedan follows at a distance. In Tangier, when they were much younger, he fed her honey cakes & mint tea. She returned the favor by licking the last hint of sweat from his body. In Lisbon, after the coup, they rented a small villa in the hills & practiced tantric yoga massaging each other's genitals with long wet strokes careful not to orgasm. It was training they both needed after all those years of unintended consequences & lovers left to rot in the road; memory forever tarnished. This morning, after a brief shower, the sky was clear & the first present arrived on time. They'd often thought to have a picnic with balloons & laughter. That was impossible now. When the door to the basement opened unexpectedly she left & was not seen again until spring. He never forgave her. It was what was expected, these being the dark years after the war. Even those who returned in one piece were broken. He's kept a diary of that time & can be found reading it to whoever will listen on the steps of the museum where he goes each day to wait. You can find him easily. He's

wearing a frayed London Fog & has dyed his hair a distinctly bright orange.
She's wearing silver slippers & smoking a thin black cigar.

After Denny Zeitlin's *BOTH/AND*

4.

Kathryn's Song

On this day. The sky. Clear. Air. Warm. Clouds drift by slowly. Nothing will be hurried. We see her feathered hat first & the basket she carries like a shopper out for a morning stroll. Only. It's mid-afternoon & she's headed for a rendezvous with a certain stranger from last week who left a gardenia on her stair & a note saying he would be waiting & wanting & much obliged & she's here to discover & whispers to herself when a man with a handsome Dane & white Stetson hat motions for her to follow & she does & now they've spread a blanket under the sprawling oak & he's opened the Chardonnay she's brought & she's buttered the bread & sliced the Brie & rests her elbow on a small pillow & the Dane lies next to him & he next to her & they sip their wine & she watches the clouds grow dark & a slight breeze chills her revelry & her eyes struggle & her hands shake & the Dane is gone & the man too & she's spilled her wine & the Brie has begun to pool & ants have found the peach she'd only nibbled & the walk home is hard & she bites her lip & drops the basket with all its trimmings in the trash & feels the first drops of the rain that is meant to clear the air but stains her cheek & runs to her mouth & she remembers there was once a song she'd sing to accompany herself on her way but the words catch in her throat & she tastes the rain & the inevitable salt.

After John Zorn's *'Masada (Live in Taipei) 1995'*

Debir

In the Sanctum Sanctorum the temple breathes.

The temple sighs. The temple erupts. Wait.

If you're unsure. The cynic knows. One foot before the other. One finger

in the wind. The whinnying

guardians of The Word. Benefactors. Since Moses, Jesus & Muhammad.

Sacrifice. Enlightenment.

Death & Resurrection. Where will we find safe landing – Justice for the

born & coming forth?

Must we bow-down our heads in humiliation?

The heron soars over the Temple Mount.

Displaced. Disoriented. Dreading the outcome.

Welcome all who will survive. Sound the trumpet.

Worry the land no more . . . Hear the anxious singing. Rapture in the

eaves. There's more to come.

Those who whittle pay a small price for solitude & peace between the ribs

of the Holy of Holies.

Debir - *Sanctum Sanctorum – Holy of Holies in Solomon's Temple*

After John Adam's *'Book Of Alleged Dances'*

Alligator Escalator

Stop the screaming. Stop the screaming. They're here, in the swamp, gorging on the bodies that sail by on the cusp of war, one by one & two by two & when the gorging stops there's the funereal silence when nature seems asleep or hiding or bored or maybe scared Yes, scared of the chomp-chomp-chomp that links every action & reaction here in The Zone where what is is not always the way it seems, where there were bodies yesterday there are only men tossing dice & women laughing up their sleeves & who can tell truth from dream & still the alligators come – in spite of the hunters & trappers & the imported pythons & . . . alligators

New Poems

2 0 1 2 – 2 0 1 6

Charleston Church Massacre - 6/17/2015

"We Forgive You"

Swept-up in a blast of heated air – one flash & another
& nowhere to run,
to hide, to breathe free . . . & he keeps
coming on
this pilfered heart, this shameless ragging,
like a lion on fire,
provoked, pissed-off, punishing, a collapsed invention
      where fear marries power,
with guns blazing the angel of death smacks his lips
slurping up a treacheries soup . . .
Speak not of justice, sanity & bigotry in one breath.
Speak not of mercy without
passion. *Do unto others as you do unto me.*
The words ring wrong.
If harmony reigns what will come to fill the vacuum?
Guilt-of-the-fathers
passed to the sons. Inbred fear of retribution. The
      Other, no longer dark but from the light comes to resurrect that
supreme fabric. *Owner. Master. Overseer.*   That sublime indifference
born of guilt – suspicion – nurturing – fomenting.
      Is there no one to speak

against the blind warrior?

     We forgive you.

It's said with conviction – tearful & full of grace. Who's

earned such a holy gift?

Tattooed across his brow a crown of thorns, swastika

     etched between his shoulder blades.

This is the time of mutilation, of dementia, of disgrace.

     Where are the voices of revolution?

Those willing to stand & be counted, unafraid of hard

choices?   The one who bears malice bears

a cataclysm too long dismissed as fated, too long

     tolerated, too long unchallenged.

"Born in blood, so blood must be spilled."

It's the way of the smuggler,

the rapist, the strangler of kids, the demon lover of

     hatred & dread.

To this we say, with all our strength – No More!

You Sent Me To Kill Or Be Killed

Staff Sgt. Robert Bales, the enigmatic figure at the center of the worst American war crime in recent memory, admitted for the first time on Wednesday deliberately killing 16 Afghan civilians last year, most of them women and children . . . Critics of America's decade of conflict in the region . . . seized on the stresses experienced in the war by soldiers like Sergeant Bales . . .

NY Times
June 5, 2013

It's Late. Night hangs heavy in Kandahar Province. Scorpions. Wood lice. A Mantis prays. Staff Sergeant Robert Bales injects his nightly dose of anabolic steroids, buckles up his gear.

Four tours in ten years. No time to reminisce, no time to dream. He's careful to climb down the ladder reserved especially for him. At the bottom is the pit, Dung Beetles scurry. His head throbs.

You've seen your buddies' shredded bodies baking in the desert sun, babies dangling dead from barbed wire, a woman blown to clots & bone by the bomb she'd wrapped around her waist.

The medic's say PTSD – The lawyers say, booze & drugs. Tonight, Robert dreams mayhem: Spirits of the brave & lost will cross the devil's river – He's locked & loaded . . .

Night goggles & high octane Wild Turkey 101. My enemies are everywhere: In their tents, behind their walls, in their gardens & in their beds. They babble in tongues, sneer & wail.

I need silence to think. My throat chokes on our renegade soup. There's nothing to be done. Extermination. I am the champion of justice, the avenger & the priest. Locked & loaded.

Bless me father for I . . . I am a missile unleashed & proud, a drone in desert camouflage. I've been sent to redeem my country's honor. I am without home, without mercy, without guilt.

Pray for me as I kneel in the sand & light my torch. Nothing is left of me. I am slag. I am heroic. I am disaster. See me for what I am, what I have been trained to be. I am a machine.

Running on fumes. Nothing matters. The mission is at hand. How many must die? & why? I am marked. Absurd. Without guile. A bomb. Fused. As intended. Poison. Catastrophe.

Collateral damage . . . It is. I am . . . What must be known . . . What must be expected.

Six AM   7-20-2012

The maimed & dead line the walk to the toilet, to the bathroom where

shaving gear rests on the green granite counter, down the polished stairs

to the kitchen, where hot tea is brewed. The maimed & dead were there

when he awoke, when he fed Buddy, the dog, when he filled the
birdfeeders.

They've been knocking on the door all day.

Most are from Aurora, Colorado, a small town east of Denver near the old
airport where not much (of note) has happened in years.

Imagine: it's midnight, bats are winging their way through star-filled skies,

Aunt Louise from Galveston arrived earlier that day & is drunk on the
porch.

Scotty, 12, the youngest of four, is sneaking peeks at the Shufuni porn site
& jacks-off into his handkerchief.

Stephanie, 20, the oldest, keeps her date in the basement where they play
at marriage & divorce for the pleasure & pain of the sex & withdrawal.

Mom's at the movies

with Samantha & Rob, the middle two,

& will never return.

Aurora, Colorado
Around Midnight 7/19/201

Sisters & Brothers

His granddaughters, Zoe & Noa, hug each other on his desk, one
protecting the other from some imagined hurt.

He rarely thinks of them this way but one glance to his right & there it is
again, the threat & the salvation.

He never had a brother or a sister. As his mother told it, they all died
before birth – those that might have been.

He never pursued them, never mourned their passing, never bothered, but
has been plagued by something -an

impulse. To hide? To bury the surviving body as they are buried? Once,
someone suggested he live

with them & they with him, that he open the door – that he pass through.
It was so easy to say – so easy . . .
*
In his dream the dead have gathered in his living room. There are five, as
she'd said. Strangers to him,

they seem to know each other & speak of him as if he had been the one to
die or, at least, cannot be found.

He moves closer to hear more clearly. They drift away, ignore his discomfort, then return, the girls

 (there are three) dress in army fatigues & stand at-ease with rifles canted to the right, the men (there are two) dress

as doctors in green scrubs & pour blood-red wine from beakers into glasses on a sideboard. He tries to tell them

he's sorry, his voice rises, his hands shake, he begins to sweat & wakes to a darkened room & the ticking of the clock.

Visitation

. . . unresting death, a whole day nearer now, . . .

From: Philip Larkin "Aubade"

It hovers, like the stink of sulfur or bad blood, wakes you in the night, squats on the edge of your bed staring into space, unmindful of your sweat, your knotted fingers or your trembling lips.

It's then the darkness closes over, leaving you gasping for air, staring into the chasm where no one speaks & nothing moves & you are now, for the first time, completely, eternally & forever alone.

In memory of Neil Lehrman

Mustering What's Left

Abracadabra & away we go into the maelstrom into the flood into the maw of the goat-of-war where bleeders roam the pastures hunting a way out & a way to believe & a way to the wayside where Uncle Charley waits in his Green Hornet disguise & Aunt What's-Her-Name snaps-up snakes for dinner & never says No to a passing grunt her being a patriot doncha know & here the wheel turns & the whistle blows & Joe with a missing leg & Artie with a missing arm toss the dice to see who goes first & around the bend with shattered knees comes the Black Reaper on his hefty Hog with all those furry fox tails & a blond fox too stroking his neck & whispering in his one good ear & here we go again down the shoot to the end of the street where the whittlers whittle & the shufflers shuffle & buttered rum is the drink of choice & chess is for keeps & here's Buddy with his perpetual grin ginning-up another cockeyed ruse for fun & games & burning the candle at both ends one in his ear & the other up his ass & away we ride to the show of shows & one for one & one for all & no one the wiser & no one to blame. It is what it is . . . doncha know.

How It Happened

Have you ever missed a step, trusted dumb luck, crafted a promise you couldn't keep?

Around midnight, the sour bells of St. Michael's warn of a crisis of faith.

Jake shuffles the deck & lays out your fortune.

Where is it written you will always be offered a second chance?

Out of the dark comes a flutter & a cough & here's Bennie & his pet hawk Max.

Suzie passes a lager down the line. Lights a Camel. Takes a deep drag.

We've been traveling these last years, we of the hit & run, we of the go & go long.

How it happened is a mystery – how she knew – how & why she escorted the corpse & then

there are all those lies. Where does it say someone will pay? Where does it say, be appeased & hang your hat here?

Her smile dazzles the warped & wanton. Score one for Robert who struggles to ejaculate.

Score one for Suzie who offers recreation or was it recuperation . . . Score one

for all who suffer silence in the face of accusation, all who whittle the brambles that clog the mind.

He's Been On This Train For Years

recruiting assassins from the ranks of the terminally ill, enduring the nightmare of the naked man who enters with a butcher knife & will not leave, dreams of seductions that will never be – while time raced past on the back of a tiger.

Some nights he remembers where & why & even what he wore: It was Tucumcari, Fire & Ice, a black leather jock. In the light of day, he tries to forget those early years: There was always cocaine & gin, sodomy & Ruthie's ruptured eyes. There was

father's war, mother's acquiescence & random acts of violence: the razor under the porch, brass knuckles & shattered glass. There was the dancer in red, around her shoulders & down one arm a shimmering boa weaving, with every gesture, every

flourish, every twist & turn would flick its tongue to taste his cheek. There were casual sightings of wives & dead babies, an enraged elephant & out of the mist his hobbled shadow. He'd once intended stalking the unsuspecting, enticing them

to his rooms where he kept the cages. When he thought
of going home, starting over & making amends, the twitching would begin
& bleeding from the rectum. There's little hope for retribution, his strength
gave out years before –

seventy three hundred days & still no peace.

A Day In The Life

At six AM she slips her one good hand under his back, leans in to kiss his
mouth. Time slips by,

like the tentative fox in heat, he takes liberties with her moist interior until
she takes him hard & twitching
in her mouth.

His turn to arrange the set & begin the anticipated rhythm. She, lazy in the
lavender bath. He,
sipping mint tea on the backstairs.

Rain has come & gone. The first robin of spring tugs at her lunch. Theirs
is a dance choreographed by anxiety & occasional hunger.

By noon the pump running in the street has done its work & he's half-way
to Viscount for a fat cabernet with a stop at Adams' for the night's gambit:

he'll roast a duck – bathe it in the essence of pomegranate laced with
balsamic vinegar.

In mid-afternoon he's at his desk wrenching words from smoky images of
nocturnal carnivals & high paid hookers straddling their pimps &

before he pricks the skin & lights the oven he downs the first shot of the day followed by the timer's buzzer &

the next & on it goes into the saffron flavored quinoa & buttered beans. She calls to assure him she is alone.

Theirs is a restless coupling.

Cornering the Corner Market

Never can tell what'll rise to the bait when you toss out a hook & line & sure enough here's where the game gets good: one by one they come from the past to join in & divvy-up the spoils & out-of-the-box pops Jesse in her birthday suit & marches right up & demands attention which she gets from all the boys & some of the girls & *Strangers Welcome* is tattooed on her ass & *Tony & Bob* are the tats on her tits & 'the trouble that follows' leaves the scene before it starts & we march to the end of the hall to spy on Ruby who entertains fellow travelers & has been known to sell reefer on the side & sure enough when the door opens there's Big Bill himself strumming his Stratocaster, Artie T on base & Joey-The-Mole on skins & at the center Bertha's passing shots of J T S Brown for old times sake & before we even blink it's our time for a good humor & a kiss on the cheek & toy poodles & all we can carry down to the car & off we go to the market where 'the rest is history' staggers past the yogurt & 'don't count your chickens' plays virtual pinball & 'fools rush in' sprints past the roasting chickens & it's not like it was & may never be again & we all chime in to say Hallelujah – just like that – in our best baritone . . . Hallelujah!

From: The Rescued Diaries Of Brother John The Vagabond

When the man with the gun stopped by for his glass of wine & a hug from La Senora we thought all would be well with our world & for a few days it was. No more mealy-mouthed muggers to worry the neighborhood & no more blood in the culverts. But that all ended just as fast as it had begun. It's now Thursday & no one is free to reminisce. In fact, no one wants to be around any of us. Oh. There's the occasional crank call & alerts. But, for the most part, we've quartered alone. Samson was the first to crack. Who can say why? He was always the most impetuous. Someone penned a note that made the rounds. There would be a rendezvous at the lake Saturday Night. Our options would be revealed. Saturday Night rolled around & I heard music in the distance a bit like that cool jazz from the 1950's. Through the light fog, I could barely make out the silhouette of a sailing ship with the lines of a schooner. It was then he came from the dunes with her on his arm. He smoked a long cheroot & she a meerschaum pipe. As they came closer he gestured for me to follow. At the ship I walked the plank & settled aboard. The dockhands tossed the lines & we were under sail. Two days later we landed at Atoll Hercules where I was to stay until my days were few & my story had become historically irrelevant . . . That's all I remember of that time & those who were in my company. Once the ship departed there were only the rowers who came in the night & the harness & the incessant chimes.

Dragonfly

2AM. Orlando, Florida . . . Omar's on the march . . . There's the oily taste of sweat or mucus or is it blood oozing over his vision. He licks his lips & grins into his phone posing in his NYPD t-shirt, gnawing his hijacked dream of martyrdom, too late for virgins in heaven, he's had his, dismissed them as awkward & flawed, lacking technique or a script worthy of a triple X. It's his last call, he wants it straight up, storms the door, levels his weapon & snuffs out forty-nine leaving fifty-three hacked & bleeding

**

There's the guy I hustled last Friday & the guy with the

Harley who'd

offered me a ride & when

I backed away smirked &

said something about temptation &

That was then . . .

Tonight.

Tonight is different.

No lies. No masks . . .Tonight's all business:

Sixty rounds a minute &

no fucking faggot's gonna get off

on me.

I'm in charge.

Calm, cool & ready to dance.

My allegiance is pledged.

I will unleash a flood of blood

over all

who tremble at my feet.

Tonight . . .Tonight

The Lieutenant's on the move. Prince of avengers. King of the mountain.

Like the Dragonfly

I glisten in my innocence.

Flash of crimson . . . Hint of lavender . . . Halo of gold

This party's just getting started.

One pass, then another. There:

One's moaning in the corner. I'll finish her off for sure &

one's rocking on his knees & you too you

motherfucker . . . & . . .

& here he pauses for a call to heaven

or is it hell

when the walls come

crashing down.

I am War. I am Mayhem. Irrelevance unleashed.

You will die in my conflagration.

Go ahead.

Ready or not

Here I am

&

Here I come.

Sordid Sequences

1

A ghost train writhes & rumbles across the valley on its way beyond the willows that line the riverbed. We've seen it before, hot metal scorching the tall grasses, its thunder driving out deer, pheasants, rabbits & all the creatures of the night. There is no map. No plan. It runs at will & chooses as it goes. Tonight is no different. The small town in its path is no match for its ferocity. One by one the houses disintegrate, shops & whiskey bars, churches & feedlots explode in a torrent of molten rock & gas. The inhabitants who've survived scramble to the hillsides where they hope to be safe from the onslaught. Some live. Some do not. The heat is intense. Steel bridges as far as a mile away collapse as their footings melt.

2

'It was never meant to happen' tells her tale with tear-filled eyes & a slight stutter. She of the priesthood. She of the Book. She of the League of Social Order. The congregation fidgets in their folding chairs & occasionally one or another will cough or take a sip from a hidden flask & on & on she goes. Seemingly, there is no reasonable explanation & when she's through, *'He of the four stars'* promises to find those who would bring this hell to our people. Promises to undo what has been done. To make up for lost time & the lies that have been spread. He seems sincere. Not like his orderly, *'He who casts the first stone'*. We've known him from years past. Racing by in his Aston Martin & secretly messing around with our women & young girls. Some say, there's a bounty on his head. As of tonight, no one has attempted to collect.

3

I am the avenger of lost causes, says *Never trust strangers*. I carry the plans to the next exposition, the future is in my backpack, salvation & brimstone marry in my wake. This is one for the books & I've read them all. I especially liked the ones with lots of sucking & fucking & lots of gore. The more the better. Understand, these are the remnants of your fractured civilization. Sorting out those worth saving is my immediate task. I'll need volunteers. Two men & two women. You'll be models for what's to come & become. &. As if an after-thought, he tweaks the cheek of Marty's mom & hauls her off to see his designs & his mysterious garden spoken about in the Big Book. In a matter of minutes, night falls on the town. No one has even hinted at sleep.

4

They've come again. Out of the mist, one with her Colobus Monkey straddling her shoulders & hissing at the man with the coiled Boa & the girl with her iguana on a leash. It's been months. We'd almost forgotten them & their irritating games of butchery & prayer. It's not often we come together to decide what will be done. Today it's Walter's turn to bang the gavel & submit the plan & he does & the sentence is death or the rack. Each must decide in turn. If all goes as before no one will submit but will chose instead to remain in the house at the end of the road, the one run by The Woman In Red who has haunted our town since the last millennium. She's known by the howling of her pet wolves & the zeal & cries of her sequestered lovers. No one has ever seen her face.

5

Only angels tread these mottled corridors of excess & grief. Not long ago, before the flood, before the famine, a man-of-war intervened. Blood spilled that day left the stain that marks our passage from be-coming to be-gone. Oh, there've been those who've tried to resurrect ambition, to open the cloistered files & resuscitate desire. Even today, not too far off, there's an encampment of *Those-who-would-be-heard*. It's only a matter of time before the trumpets sound & the cycle will begin again. What will it take to finally break tradition & honor again the common good?

6

Score one for the overseers & flag-men of opportunity gone amuck:

He's squandered justice & her generous gift of reclamation. His path is mottled with the skeletons of mocking monkeys & his mother's reluctance. From the corners of history, indulgence cries for forgiveness. As he sweeps, the leaves rustle like his fractious complaints, he's like some minor player cast to hell & lost in the shuffle. Not one to war against hypocrisy, his complaints fall like flares on snow. There must be a better way, another path less traveled. Here, if I offer my hand you must take it & what about her & her conceited fiancé? Do you still insist on going alone, into the furnace & down the drain. Even the hound has learned to relish the comfort of a bed & predictable sustenance. Try not to bleed all over the sofa.

About the Poet

Born in Chicago, Illinois, Roger Aplon was a founder and managing editor of Chicago's CHOICE Magazine with John Logan & Aaron Siskind. He has had twelve books published: One of prose: Intimacies & eleven of poetry (most recently Improvisation: Poetic Impressions From Contemporary Music). He often reads his work with musicians from the Avant-Garde ensembles Wormhole (In Yokohama & Tokyo Japan) & the Trummerflora Collective (San Diego, CA). In the course of his career he's been awarded prizes and honors including an Arts Fellowship from the Helene Wurlitzer Foundation in Taos, New Mexico. After an eight year writing retreat in Barcelona Spain, he now makes his home in Beacon, New York where he edits & publishes a poetry magazine: 'Waymark – Voices of the Valley' & has assembled his first collection of 'Selected & New Poems' You can read and hear examples of his work at: www.rogeraplon.com

About the Press

Unsolicited Press is a small publishing house based in the Pacific Northwest. The team has published over sixty titles and continues to seek astonishing and vibrant poetry, fiction, and nonfiction. More can be learned about Unsolicited Press at www.unsolicitedpress.com.